FROM THE ZABBALA'S CART

DINA EL DESSOUKY

Published by Akashic Books
©2019 Dina El Dessouky

ISBN: 978-1-61775-741-9

Printed in China
First printing

Akashic Books
Brooklyn, New York, USA
Ballydehob, Co. Cork, Ireland
Twitter: @AkashicBooks
Facebook: AkashicBooks
E-mail: info@akashicbooks.com
Website: www.akashicbooks.com

African Poetry Book Fund
Prairie Schooner
University of Nebraska
110 Andrews Hall
Lincoln, Nebraska 68588

TABLE OF CONTENTS

PREFACE
by Fady Joudah

The most compelling poetry is nomadic, restless—not in a hunter-gatherer manner where the self is obsessed with catalog for mere conquest, but in a spiritual way where what's possessed is wholly experienced, lived with, before it is let go. In modern parlance, and in Dina El Dessouky's words, her roaming poems are concerned with collecting scraps, discarded objects, daily trash (*zibala*, in Arabic). Fully or partially consumed, recyclable or not, this trash lives along the semiconductor highway that is our contemporary lives. And with her gift for the universal, the magic in her art is doubled. Feel through these lines on a bed of nails, as the title of the opening poem declares; the chemical is never far from the sarcophagus.

> Noble is she
>
> who remains anchored
> to plaster and asbestos
> year after year
> [. . .]
> who eases into
> coffins
> but never dies.

Dina El Dessouky's background is an amalgam of an African Arab (Egyptian) experience and a Western one. The former manifests itself in many cultural references and through a handful of harmonious transliterations in Egyptian dialect. The Western component of her identity also shares peoples and communities that she's closely connected with and influenced by. Kamau Braithwaite comes to mind along with others mentioned or alluded to in these poems: "I binge and simmer in the pain / as I hear Marvin Gaye sing, / 'How Sweet It Is to Be Loved By You.'"

This parliament of belonging, through which the poet grants herself one foot inside many doors—an openness, solidarity, filiation, and affiliation that is palpably great within her—manifests itself in myriad forms. In driving tonally rich rhythms that are a delight for the imagination, El Dessouky oscillates between humor and satire, wildness and love, intelligence within and beyond reason:

> Lover, I never knew
> earplugs before
> we met
> [...]
> and you are
> barrel-chested.
> Now my canals
>
> are caulked
> with foamy .45s
> slick like
>
> Agent Orange,
> and active shooters
> roam my psyche
>
> nightly like love
> sick puppies
> Lover, I met another
>
> barrel-chested
> man last night.
> He exploded

a cloud
of feathers
in me

and I knew again
how deer graze at dawn
and crickets rub limbs,

how softly my
parents spoke before they
both fell prey

to the insufferable heat.

I want to return to transliteration for a moment. Many of us have
come to think of it as a form, or performance, of identity politics and, to an
extent, it is, as it should be. However, there is another quality to transliteration that can illuminate how El Dessouky journeys within the sublime or
uncanny.

Her Arabic is directly linked to "the heresy / of remembering" and the
energies of a most private tongue. Her fluency in Arabic may be limited,
but it drives her being to sing those energies into the liminal zone, the
brackish water of language. Yet hers is a seamless, bidirectional current:
from river to estuary to sea and the other way around. El Dessouky's Arabic
(undetectable, undeclared, or transliterated) frames the familial (nuclear and
communal, Egyptian and American) and the psychological forces they hold.

"A Surfboard Named Fatma," the last poem in this collection, contains
no transliteration but exhibits the panoply within the poet's creative home.
Her propensity for the panoramic is a mosaic of ecstatic details that parades
us around the circles of her song. At heart, she's a poet of praise, and "we

buckle . . . under the weight" of that joy as we revel in the holiness of poly-
urethane and ritual dance. "Bless us all, that we may atone," indeed:

> Fatma, O sacred vessel,
>> his ninety-nine names stir in your womb,
>> unmarred by my navel
>> and sands that cling
>> to bare soles and
>> half-naked beachcombers,
>> raisins
>> and virgin foreheads.

> Fatma, O holy prayer rug,
>> might I borrow your eyes
>> to see
>> the Merciful, the Compassionate
>> in box jelly tentacles
>> and starving seabirds?
> [. . .]
> Fatma, we dance graceful sun hawk dances,
>> cast shadows that resemble sharks beneath us.

> Fatma, [. . .]
>> my feet massage your polyurethane marrow.

> Fatma, [   ]

> Bless us all, that we may atone.

NAILS

Noble is she

who remains anchored
to plaster and asbestos
year after year

who is overshadowed
by forced smiles and
fragile beauty

who bears the weight of
the world on her head
like a clay jug

who turned
this house
into a home

who bends
when carelessly hammered
but never crucifies

who eases into
coffins
but never dies.

WEIGHTS

When you let them go

stack lovers
like mattresses,
box springs, and
laundered sheets.

Stack lovers
like pancakes
dripping in
morning after syrup;
even the soiled and stained
demand dignity
before their next crush.

Stack lovers
like old photos;
shove them into a drawer
but never burn them.

Stack lovers
like tiny gemstones
strung along
an orgy of necklaces
over the wrong chakra;
cast them away like fish fry
and cleanse after touching.
Their price is too high.

Stack lovers
like corrugated cardboard
on garbage day;
outside of
the box,
we might not cut
new lovers down.

Stack lovers
like barbell weights
in a junkyard.
Uplift them;
set them aside
in a shopping cart
and wait for the right person
to check them out.

Stack lovers
like cotton panties,
menstrual cloths,
chux pads, or
receiving blankets.

Stack your softness
and it will grow.

EARPLUGS

Lover, I never knew
earplugs before
we met

but I penetrate
sleep and wakefulness
like goose down

and you are
barrel-chested.
Now my canals

are caulked
with foamy .45s
slick like

Agent Orange,
and active shooters
roam my psyche

nightly like love
sick puppies.
Lover, I met another

barrel-chested
man last night.
He exploded

a cloud
of feathers
in me

and I knew again
how deer graze at dawn
and crickets rub limbs,

how softly my
parents spoke before they
both fell prey

to the insufferable heat.
Lover, last night
my earplugs

slipped out

but I found them again
crushed under the weight
of a leavening moon.

BROKEN MIRROR

Her nose
is a shard
of silver plated glass
that a witch broke
with one hard
cold press
of her olive eyes
into a mirror.

When it broke
the witch cried
a monsoon

at the laughing mosaic of

   barbed wire

       spidery lashes

  pocked brows

    crow's feet

  mottled browns

      and hooked beaks

a clan of hyenas
watching the lioness
gorge on her

spellbinding beauty

charcoal gray and pearling

like a midsummer storm cloud
bereaving the land
of her thirst.

FIRST FOOD

Before
pizza, fish sticks, hamburgers, chicken nuggets, and tater tots;
before
chocolate milk,
before
warak einab,
and even before
fuul mudammas bil aish baladi
came
Mama's breasts.

Mama's breasts
were small
before I took them
from her.

Mine are large now,
filling with
colostrum,
soon to be
milk machines.

When Mama's breasts were
full of milk
I took them from her
without realizing
she had little support.

Not yet conscious

I turned her breasts to stone.

She could no longer pump
the raw, tender
pieces of dried meat
and so she filled them
with a hormone
to make them stop
hurting her.

And that was when
I stole one from her,
lopped off the first slab of flesh
several months after
I came out of her body.

She found the lump.
She was sure it was from the pills,
never once blaming
her carnivorous child.

I look at my breasts
with a smirk in the mirror
and ripe cantaloupe stare back,
begging to be suckled.

Mama paid with her breasts first,
then paid for formula,
clothes,
a private room for my budding bosom,
college.

By sleeping on the closet floor,
by buying
canned,
generic brand, and
frozen foods,
Mama went to work
and gave me
a fresh start.

HOLIDAY CANDY

My tongue muscles through
the screams of orangutans
and burning trees.

My teeth crush
the spines of children
enslaved and free.

My throat chokes back
the suffocating villages
of our ash-coated planet.

I binge and simmer in the pain
as I hear Marvin Gaye sing,
"How Sweet It Is to Be Loved By You."

HAIR TIES

1.

The day my hair tie broke
I yelled, "Fuck!"
and cracked a wry smile
at the student evaluation
that read "unprofessional."

I couldn't contain myself.

I paid five cents for it,
but breaking it
cost me my dignity.

I couldn't contain myself.

2.

The day my hair tie broke
my infant grabbed a fistful
of stray curls,
tiny vice grip fingers
holding fast to her roots.

3./٣

The day my hair tie broke

the police pulled me over.
I wondered if I'd get taken
in;
I wondered if I'd get taken
out.

.٤/4.

The day my hair tie broke
I heard my mother's voice
beat a frantic rhythm
inside my skull—
"Limmi sha3rik, ya bint"

—but felt sexy again
for a second.

.٥

The day my hair tic broke
I thought to myself, "Ana hummara,"
as my locks scrambled
to swat their gnat-like calls
of "ya sharbat, ya 'amar"
from my ears.

I failed to lick clean
the unsavory clicks on teeth,
accidental presses

in Khan el Khalili
passageways.

6.

The day my hair tie broke
their dirty blonde mouths
yelled, "Brown Sugar,"
and I offered myself—
unsifted.

When I got home
I purged, holding back
my own hair.

7./.٧

Because
this body unleashed
is a threat,
a liability
to itself.

HAIR BRUSH

When my iron coils
broke half your teeth
I made sure to leave you

extra baksheesh
O Cairo cab driver
on the Autobahn

I know how much
you miss your
crooked streets.

FOOD SCRAPS FROM THE DINING ROOM

for Matthew Shenoda

"Yanhar eswad! Beytik mazballeh,"
my mother laments,
her naked foot
saturated with milk
from my dining room floor.

Must remind you of home,
I think to myself,
but hold my tongue.

Mother, I am the worst kind of human.
I plague your house with
Bilharzia.

I plague your house with
the heresy
of remembering.

Now that I am a mother
I am ravenous and wasteful
in the worst ways.

For dinner I microwave
clumps of makarona
foraged from the freezer section,

and like me

my infant is ravenous and
turns fresh produce into confetti

                three times a day.

I force feed the compost
waxing gibbous oranges
tainted by my eldest's tiny
vampire teeth three times a day.

             We three daughters
            ravenous and wasteful
watch ravens caw their secrets

on the wire outside our dining room.
I curse them—
"Tattle Tales! Snitches! Ya Ghuraaba!"

                      And if
            the Poet's Great-Grandmother is right,
                      and if

                  God will make me
                    pick up salt
                one grain at a time

                with my eyelashes,[1]

---

1 after Matthew Shenoda's poem "New Cairo"

then, Mother,
may I be reborn ravenous
picking up each stray crumb and morsel

with my nonexistent eyelashes
as I squirm through
your parched earth?

Mother,
may I be reborn ravenous
to blacken your soil once more

with my castings, even if it takes a billion years
and I die and am reborn again
each time

trying a little harder?

TICKET TO MASR

In my palm
lies

a ticket.

Some days
it reads,
San Francisco to Cairo,
one way—

a return to—

as if I didn't fear crossing
oceans
and Cairo streets.

As if home
   were a Ra'asa
   with the antique frame
   of a date palm,
   rustling her gold coins
   to El Sahara's beating hawa,

   not a bead of sweat on her forehead.

I fear
my palms lie
dormant and defeated
by batons cracking phalanges

and pigeon toes.

I fear
my palms lie,
that our hijacked minds
stand no chance
of making it home
in the first place.

I fear my palms lie.

How well do you know your palms?

I get lost
staring into each crevice, at each ring, round each groove,
whispering prayers into epidermal cross hashing
that God and our DNA put there.

I get lost
dwelling in lands

as alien

as my frostbitten knuckles,
the blood siphoned from
their purple majesty,
yet climb
down into pale
nail beds
for the comfort

of knowing my ochre hands
can know bare brown thighs
on warm afternoons at the park.

I fear a return to covered thighs;
"Inti houra,"
Mama always said,
her disappointment veiled in summer fog.

"Haram 3alayki!"
their eyes would say,
scouring her knees

so raw she never returned.

I fear a return
to a land
no longer
black nor fertile,
no tilapia
to shelter our
futures in their lyrical mouths,
no scarabs
to sift through the rubble
and bear the fruit of our future.

I fear a return
to palms
that face the sky
in a haze
of taxi smoke and sheesha,
one crowded city
choking on its own breath.

My palms persist.
My palms speak truth.

My return ticket lies.
I cannot return.

FAVORITE CHAIR

The Carpenter wanted a daughter
gamda, qawwaya like herself
with the thick skin of an oak
under her polished surface,

> a daughter solid and strong enough
> to fell a tree with her hands
> and craft from its wood

> a chair upon which
> Madame could rest her back
> after a hard day's work.

The Carpenter's favorite chairs
adorned Victorian salons,
plump and dainty
thighs boasting
coy question marks
over their curled toes.

Madame planted a tree,
fancying apples
of rosy flesh
smooth and crisp
that fell not too far from her own.

> But Madame got a Willow
> laden with silty water.

Madame didn't know
        that every time
her head throbbed
the Willow would too
and pare her skin;
        that every time
Madame sought shelter from
the Cairene sun
that stalked her,
        the Willow would uproot herself,
        bent under the weight of her
        cascading tendrils
        to offer Madame her shade.

But Madame had little use
for idling beneath
cool, weeping leaves
                and chopped the Willow
                down

with a butcher's precision for limbs
and choice cuts,
rubbed the wood clean
with 50 grit,
embalmed it with varnish,
                        but was surprised
                        that when she rested
                        her burdens
                        against the Willow's bones,

        she drowned

the Chair
in stagnant tears,

sap gathering at the corners of
her splintered eyes.

DEER SKIN DRUM

after Yusef Komunyakaa

When I strike you

I hear my Great
great
great
great
grandfather's feet
in that moment before
his arrow splayed the gazelle.

For my daughters
and theirs
again and again
and again and
again,

across seven continents
and thirteen moons,

     I split open
          her throat
               and leap out.

BROOMS

Everyone knows
we're

      the witches

ride
or die

      bitches,

but few know
why we

      cackle,

that our
laughs

      crackle

from years of
dust on straw;

we bristle
when we're

      swept under the rug or
      denied a seat at the table.

Incensed,
we

      push it,
      fingers nursing salt and pepper babies.

We light
our lungs

      on fire and wave
      frankincense, copal, sweetgrass, and myrhh:

sage braids.
We stand

      on end
      knowing

              how bad
             the world needs
              our work.

A SURFBOARD NAMED FATMA

Fatma, you are neon pink
      highlighting the brightness of our days.

Daughter of the Prophet—peace be upon him—
      with you
      each paddle stroke
      is a prayer for sick dogs
      and great
      whites.

Fatma, O sacred vessel,
      his ninety-nine names stir in your womb,
      unmarred by my navel
      and sands that cling
      to bare soles and
      half-naked beachcombers,
      raisins
      and virgin foreheads.

Fatma, O holy prayer rug,
      might I borrow your eyes
      to see
      the Merciful, the Compassionate
      in box jelly tentacles
      and starving seabirds?

Fatma, I seek your counsel:

            Guide me over the wave's puckered lip.

Guide me over submerged rocks and churning boils.

Guide me through the tunnels of springtime upwelling.
Guide me through my struggles.

Guide me beyond stillbirths at the barrel's mouth.
Guide me into eternity with your sage palm.

Fatma, we dance graceful sun hawk dances,
      cast shadows that resemble sharks beneath us.

Fatma, you shine like the moon in all her phases
      and like her I
      caress your seamless haunches daily;
      my feet massage your polyurethane marrow.

Fatma, when you buckle one day
      under the weight of our praise,
      bless our poisoned mother
         in spite of your own withering bones.

Bless us all, that we may atone.

NOTES

Zabbala: Garbage Collector (title, feminine)

warak einab: stuffed grape leaves

fuul mudammas bil aish baladi: mashed fava beans in sauce with flat bread

Limmi sha3rik, ya bint: put your hair up, girl

Ana hummara: I'm a donkey

ya sharbat: syrup

ya 'amar: hey you, moon

Yanhar eswad: a hyperbole; literally, "Oh Black Day"

Beytik mazballeh: your house is a dump

makarona: noodles

Ya Ghuraaba: you strangers

Ra'asa: folk dancer

hawa: wind

Inti houra: you're free

Haram 3alayki: shame on you

gamda: solid

qawwaya: strong

ACKNOWLEDGMENTS

Many thanks to the editors of the following publications in which these poems or previous versions of them originally appeared:

Mizna (print)—"First Food" (15.1, 2014)

Anomaly (online): "Hair Ties," "Hair Brush," "Favorite Chair" (May 2018)

I am deeply grateful to the following poets for their generous mentorship: Chris Abani, Elmaz Abinader, Kwame Dawes, Oliver de la Paz, Fady Joudah, and Matthew Shenoda. Thank you also to the VONA/Voices of Our Nations Arts Foundation, the Quest Writer's Conference, Las Dos Brujas Writers' Workshops, and the Santa Cruz Recycled Art Program, for offering the creative spaces within which I first wrote or rediscovered many of the poems in this chapbook. Finally, my heartfelt thanks go out to the African Poetry Book Fund and the entire team at Akashic Books for continuing to make the publication of this chapbook series possible.